Instant
File-Folder Games
for Math

by Linda Ward Beech

SCHOLASTIC
PROFESSIONAL BOOKS

New York • Toronto • London • Auckland • Sydney
Mexico City • New Delhi • Hong Kong

Cover design by Jaime Lucero

Interior design by Sydney Wright

Cover and interior illustrations by Rusty Fletcher

ISBN 0-439-13730-6

Contents

To the Teacher

Instant File-Folder Games for Math offers an engaging and fun way to reinforce important math skills. Just photocopy and color the game boards, glue them inside file folders, and you've got ten instant math-center activities! The games are a snap to set up and store: Each game has a handy pocket on the front of the file folder in which to store the reproducible directions and game parts. Kids will have fun as they practice adding with Nine in a Hive, subtracting with Fun at the Fair, counting money with Spend 'n Earn, multiplying with Multiplication Mountain, and much more.

Playing games is a great way to motivate children of all learning styles to practice math skills. There are a variety of ways you can use the games to meet the needs of your students. Store the games in a math center and encourage students to play before or after school, during free time, or when they have finished other tasks. You can also send games home for students to play with family members and friends. Use the Extending the Game suggestions for each game to continue to build students' skills and interest.

How to Use This Book

Each game comes with an introductory page for the teacher that provides a suggestion for introducing the game, step-by-step directions for assembling the game, and suggestions to extend learning. Following this page are the reproducible parts for the game: a label for the file-folder tab; a pocket for the front of the file folder in which to store the game parts; directions for the students that explain how to play the game; and a game board. Some games also include cards, playing pieces, an answer key, and a spinner. To enhance the game board and playing pieces, you may wish to have students color them. Some games include specific coloring directions.

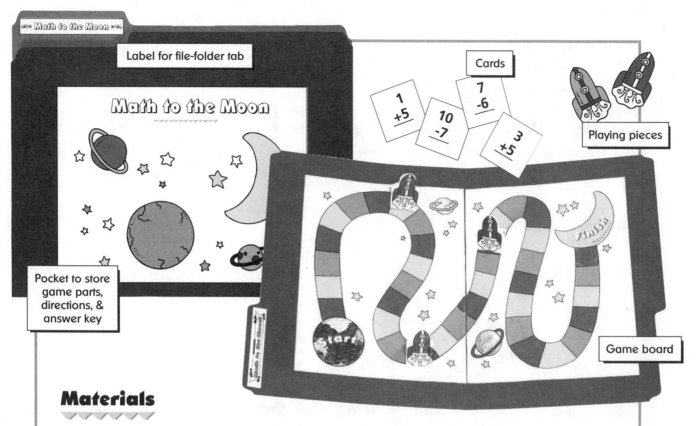

Label for file-folder tab

Math to the Moon

Cards

1
+5

10
-7

7
-6

3
+5

Playing pieces

Pocket to store game parts, directions, & answer key

Game board

Materials

In addition to the reproducible game pages, you'll need the following:

▲ 10 file folders   ▲ glue or rubber cement

▲ scissors   ▲ paper clips

▲ paper fasteners   ▲ crayons or colored pencils

▲ tape   ▲ dice or number cubes (reproducible on page 64)

▲ playing pieces (chips, beans, pennies, colored squares of paper, or playing pieces from a board game)

Tips

⊙ Laminate the game pieces for sturdiness and durability.

⊙ Conduct mini-lessons to review the skills required in each game.

⊙ Model how to play each game for students.

⊙ Give children suggestions to determine the order in which players take turns, such as rolling a die and taking turns in numerical order.

Storage Ideas

Keep the file-folder games in any of these places:

▲ math resource center   ▲ vertical file tray

▲ file box   ▲ file cabinet

▲ bookshelf

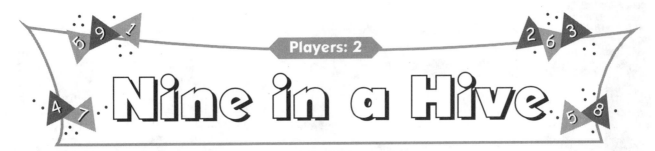

Nine in a Hive

Objective: This game provides practice in adding numbers up to 9.

Introduction

Have students practice counting up to 9 with counters. Explain that in this game, children will be adding the numbers on the bees.

Assembling the Game

 Duplicate and cut out the file-folder label and pocket on page 7. Glue the label onto the tab of a file folder. Tape the pocket on three sides to the outside front of the folder.

 Duplicate and cut out the directions and answer key on page 8. Make two copies of the bee cards on page 9 so that you have 40 cards in all. Cut out the bee cards and invite students to color them. When the game is not in use, store these items in the pocket on the front of the folder.

 Duplicate and cut out the beehive game board on pages 10 and 11. Invite students to color it, and then glue it onto the inside of the folder.

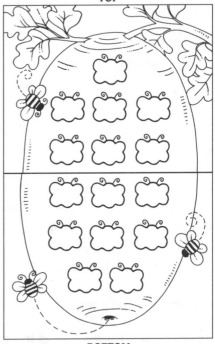

TOP

BOTTOM

Extending the Game

⊙ Invite children to tell stories about the bees that are "buzzing" out of the hive.

⊙ Have students use the cards for other addition activities. For example, place the shuffled cards facedown on a table and have children pick two cards and add the numbers on them.

Nine in a Hive

▶▶ Nine in a Hive ▶▶

Nine in a Hive

Directions for Play
(for 2 players)

1. One player is the dealer and shuffles the bee cards. The dealer places the first 15 cards faceup in the 15 spaces on the beehive. The dealer places the rest of the cards facedown in a pile near the game board.

2. The other player goes first. The player removes from the board two cards that add up to 9 and keeps them. Then the dealer chooses two cards that add up to 9.

3. Play continues in this way with each player taking turns. When there are no more cards on the board that add up to 9, a player takes the top card from the pile. If the player can add that card to one on the board to make 9, the player keeps both cards. If not, the card is added to a space on the game board. (If there are no cards left on the board, place two cards from the pile on the board and continue playing as before.)

4. The game is over when all the cards have been drawn from the pile. The player with the most cards wins.

Answer Key

1 + 8	2 + 7	3 + 6	4 + 5	0 + 9
8 + 1	7 + 2	6 + 3	5 + 4	9 + 0

Nine in a Hive

Bee Cards

Nine in a Hive

Game Board

Trim off this strip and attach to page 11.

Nine in a Hive

Game Board

Instant File-Folder Games for Math   Scholastic Professional Books

Attach to page 10 here.

Nine in a Hive

Game Board

Apple Adding

Objective: This game provides practice in adding sums up to 18.

Introduction

Review with students addition problems up to 18, especially those that use two-digit numbers. Explain that in this game students will be adding the numbers on the apples.

Assembling the Game

1. Duplicate and cut out the file-folder label and pocket on page 13. Glue the label onto the tab of a file folder. Tape the pocket on three sides to the outside front of the folder.

2. Duplicate and cut out the directions and two sets of the apple markers on pages 14–15. (You will need 40 apples all together.) When the game is not in use, store these items in the pocket on the front of the folder.

3. Duplicate and cut out the game board on pages 16 and 17. Glue it onto the inside of the folder.

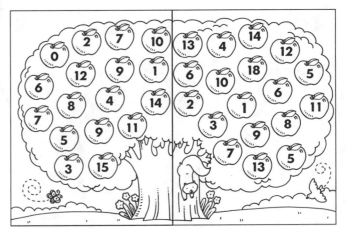

4. Invite students to color the apple markers and game board. Have students color 20 apples green and 20 apples red.

   NOTE: If necessary, children can use a calculator to check their answers.

Extending the Game

⊙ On a separate sheet of paper, have students write down each addition problem they complete on the game board.

Apple Adding
Label and Pocket

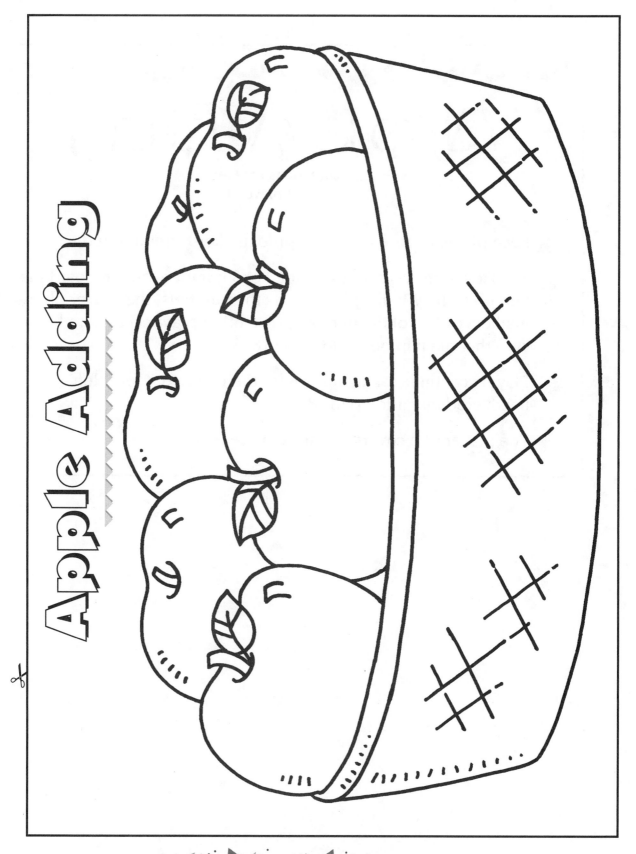

Apple Adding

Apple Adding

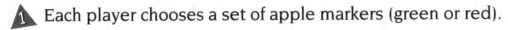

Apple Adding

Directions for Play
(for 2 players)

1. Each player chooses a set of apple markers (green or red).

2. To take a turn, a player looks for 2 or 3 numbers on the board that add up to 18. When a player finds the numbers, the player places markers on top of the numbers. The other player checks to be sure that the numbers add up to 18.

3. Players continue taking turns until there are no apples left uncovered that add up to 18.

4. The player who covers the most apples wins.

Apple Adding

Apple Markers

Apple Adding

Game Board

Trim off this strip and attach to page 17.

Apple Adding

Game Board

Instant File-Folder Games for Math Scholastic Professional Books

Players: 2–3

Fun at the Fair

Objective: This game provides practice in subtracting numbers up to 18.
Some problems involve regrouping.

Introduction

You may wish to have students review subtraction facts up to 18. Remind students that the minus sign means "subtract."

Assembling the Game

1. Duplicate and cut out the file-folder label and pocket on page 19. Glue the label onto the tab of a file folder. Tape the pocket on three sides to the outside front of the folder.

2. Duplicate and cut out the directions, answer key, and two sets of the cards on pages 20–21. When the game is not in use, store these items in the pocket on the front of the folder.

3. To make markers, cut small paper squares in three colors (15 of each color). These should be large enough to cover the prizes on the board. You could also use beans, chips, pennies, or other small manipulatives.

4. Duplicate and cut out the game board on pages 22–23. Invite students to color the game board, and then glue it onto the inside of the folder.

Extending the Game

⊙ Have students make up stories about the prizes that they "win" at the fair.

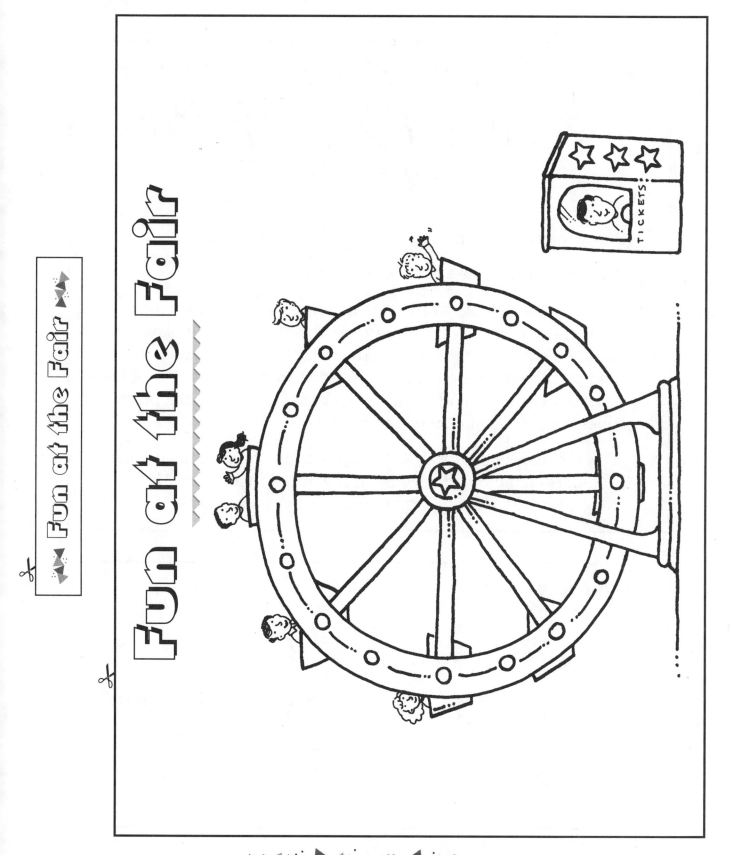

Fun at the Fair

✂ ▸▸ Fun at the Fair ▸▸

Fun at the Fair

Directions for Play
(for 2–3 players)

1 Place the cards facedown in a pile near the game board.

2 Each player chooses a set of colored markers.

3 The first player picks a card from the pile, shows the card to the others, and then answers the subtraction problem. The player then looks for a prize number on the board that matches the answer and places a marker on it. If a player does not answer the problem correctly or cannot find a prize with the same number, the player does not place a marker on the board.

4 Play continues in this way with players taking turns until all prize numbers on the board have been covered with markers. The player with the most prizes (markers on the board) wins.

Answer Key

A. $\begin{array}{r} 18 \\ -\ 9 \\ \hline 9 \end{array}$	B. $\begin{array}{r} 18 \\ -\ 5 \\ \hline 13 \end{array}$	C. $\begin{array}{r} 17 \\ -\ 9 \\ \hline 8 \end{array}$	D. $\begin{array}{r} 17 \\ -\ 7 \\ \hline 10 \end{array}$	E. $\begin{array}{r} 16 \\ -\ 7 \\ \hline 9 \end{array}$	F. $\begin{array}{r} 16 \\ -\ 5 \\ \hline 11 \end{array}$	G. $\begin{array}{r} 15 \\ -\ 9 \\ \hline 6 \end{array}$
H. $\begin{array}{r} 15 \\ -\ 8 \\ \hline 7 \end{array}$	I. $\begin{array}{r} 15 \\ -\ 6 \\ \hline 9 \end{array}$	J. $\begin{array}{r} 14 \\ -\ 3 \\ \hline 11 \end{array}$	K. $\begin{array}{r} 14 \\ -\ 7 \\ \hline 7 \end{array}$	L. $\begin{array}{r} 13 \\ -\ 4 \\ \hline 9 \end{array}$	M. $\begin{array}{r} 13 \\ -\ 5 \\ \hline 8 \end{array}$	N. $\begin{array}{r} 13 \\ -\ 7 \\ \hline 6 \end{array}$
O. $\begin{array}{r} 13 \\ -\ 8 \\ \hline 5 \end{array}$	P. $\begin{array}{r} 12 \\ -\ 9 \\ \hline 3 \end{array}$	Q. $\begin{array}{r} 12 \\ -\ 6 \\ \hline 6 \end{array}$	R. $\begin{array}{r} 12 \\ -\ 8 \\ \hline 4 \end{array}$	S. $\begin{array}{r} 11 \\ -\ 4 \\ \hline 7 \end{array}$	T. $\begin{array}{r} 11 \\ -\ 6 \\ \hline 5 \end{array}$	

Fun at the Fair

Subtraction Cards

A. 18 -9 ___	B. 18 -5 ___	C. 17 -9 ___	D. 17 -7 ___
E. 16 -7 ___	F. 16 -5 ___	G. 15 -9 ___	H. 15 -8 ___
I. 15 -6 ___	J. 14 -3 ___	K. 14 -7 ___	L. 13 -4 ___
M. 13 -5 ___	N. 13 -7 ___	O. 13 -8 ___	P. 12 -9 ___
Q. 12 -6 ___	R. 12 -8 ___	S. 11 -4 ___	T. 11 -6 ___

Fun at the Fair

Game Board

Trim off this strip and attach to page 23.

Fun at the Fair

Game Board

Attach to page 22 here.

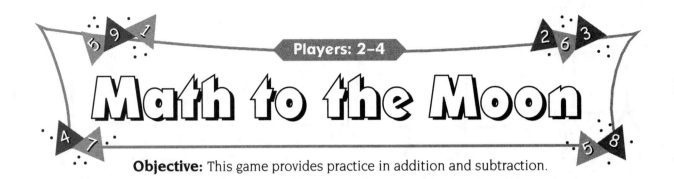

Math to the Moon

Objective: This game provides practice in addition and subtraction.

Introduction

Have students review addition and subtraction facts. Remind students that the plus sign means "add" and the minus sign means "subtract."

Assembling the Game

 Duplicate and cut out the file-folder label and pocket on page 30. Glue the label onto the tab of a file folder. Tape the pocket on three sides to the outside front of the folder.

 Duplicate and cut out the directions, cards, and answer key on pages 25–27. When the game is not in use, store these items in the pocket on the front of the folder.

 Make four copies of the playing piece on page 27. Color each playing piece a different color. Fold the tabs so that the pieces stand up.

 Duplicate and cut out the game board on pages 28–29. Invite students to color the game board, and then glue it onto the inside of the folder.

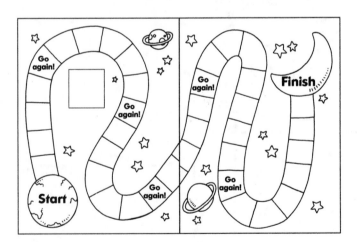

Extending the Game

⊙ Have students make up more cards with different addition and subtraction facts to use in the game.

⊙ Use the game cards as flash cards.

Math to the Moon

Directions for Play
(for 2–4 players)

1. Place the cards facedown on the board. Each player chooses a playing piece and places it on Start.

2. Players take turns picking a card and adding or subtracting. If they add, they move ahead that number of spaces. If they subtract, they must move back that number of spaces. Players can only move back as far as the Start space. (If a player in the Start space chooses a subtraction card, he or she cannot move on that turn.) Players put the cards at the bottom of the pile.

3. The first player to reach Finish is the winner.

Answer Key

1. $\begin{array}{r}3\\+3\\\hline6\end{array}$	2. $\begin{array}{r}12\\-9\\\hline3\end{array}$	3. $\begin{array}{r}1\\+4\\\hline5\end{array}$	4. $\begin{array}{r}5\\+0\\\hline5\end{array}$	5. $\begin{array}{r}7\\-5\\\hline2\end{array}$	6. $\begin{array}{r}2\\+5\\\hline7\end{array}$	7. $\begin{array}{r}4\\+4\\\hline8\end{array}$	8. $\begin{array}{r}11\\-9\\\hline2\end{array}$	9. $\begin{array}{r}2\\+2\\\hline4\end{array}$	10. $\begin{array}{r}9\\-8\\\hline1\end{array}$	11. $\begin{array}{r}6\\+2\\\hline8\end{array}$	12. $\begin{array}{r}10\\-8\\\hline2\end{array}$
13. $\begin{array}{r}2\\+3\\\hline5\end{array}$	14. $\begin{array}{r}0\\+6\\\hline6\end{array}$	15. $\begin{array}{r}6\\+3\\\hline9\end{array}$	16. $\begin{array}{r}7\\-6\\\hline1\end{array}$	17. $\begin{array}{r}3\\+5\\\hline8\end{array}$	18. $\begin{array}{r}5\\+1\\\hline6\end{array}$	19. $\begin{array}{r}9\\-7\\\hline2\end{array}$	20. $\begin{array}{r}12\\-8\\\hline4\end{array}$	21. $\begin{array}{r}6\\+1\\\hline7\end{array}$	22. $\begin{array}{r}2\\+0\\\hline2\end{array}$	23. $\begin{array}{r}3\\+4\\\hline7\end{array}$	24. $\begin{array}{r}7\\-3\\\hline4\end{array}$
25. $\begin{array}{r}4\\+3\\\hline7\end{array}$	26. $\begin{array}{r}4\\+2\\\hline6\end{array}$	27. $\begin{array}{r}1\\+0\\\hline1\end{array}$	28. $\begin{array}{r}6\\-4\\\hline2\end{array}$	29. $\begin{array}{r}3\\+1\\\hline4\end{array}$	30. $\begin{array}{r}10\\-7\\\hline3\end{array}$	31. $\begin{array}{r}0\\+3\\\hline3\end{array}$	32. $\begin{array}{r}2\\+1\\\hline3\end{array}$	33. $\begin{array}{r}1\\+5\\\hline6\end{array}$	34. $\begin{array}{r}8\\-8\\\hline0\end{array}$	35. $\begin{array}{r}11\\-8\\\hline3\end{array}$	36. $\begin{array}{r}5\\+4\\\hline9\end{array}$

Math to the Moon

Cards

1. $\begin{array}{r} 3 \\ +3 \\ \hline \end{array}$	2. $\begin{array}{r} 12 \\ -9 \\ \hline \end{array}$	3. $\begin{array}{r} 1 \\ +4 \\ \hline \end{array}$	4. $\begin{array}{r} 5 \\ +0 \\ \hline \end{array}$
5. $\begin{array}{r} 7 \\ -5 \\ \hline \end{array}$	6. $\begin{array}{r} 2 \\ +5 \\ \hline \end{array}$	7. $\begin{array}{r} 4 \\ +4 \\ \hline \end{array}$	8. $\begin{array}{r} 11 \\ -9 \\ \hline \end{array}$
9. $\begin{array}{r} 2 \\ +2 \\ \hline \end{array}$	10. $\begin{array}{r} 9 \\ -8 \\ \hline \end{array}$	11. $\begin{array}{r} 6 \\ +2 \\ \hline \end{array}$	12. $\begin{array}{r} 10 \\ -8 \\ \hline \end{array}$
13. $\begin{array}{r} 2 \\ +3 \\ \hline \end{array}$	14. $\begin{array}{r} 0 \\ +6 \\ \hline \end{array}$	15. $\begin{array}{r} 6 \\ +3 \\ \hline \end{array}$	16. $\begin{array}{r} 7 \\ -6 \\ \hline \end{array}$
17. $\begin{array}{r} 3 \\ +5 \\ \hline \end{array}$	18. $\begin{array}{r} 5 \\ +1 \\ \hline \end{array}$	19. $\begin{array}{r} 9 \\ -7 \\ \hline \end{array}$	20. $\begin{array}{r} 12 \\ -8 \\ \hline \end{array}$

Math to the Moon

Cards and Playing Pieces

21.	22.	23.	24.
6 +1	2 +0	3 +4	7 -3

25.	26.	27.	28.
4 +3	4 +2	1 +0	6 -4

29.	30.	31.	32.
3 +1	10 -7	0 +3	2 +1

33.	34.	35.	36.
1 +5	8 -8	11 -8	5 +4

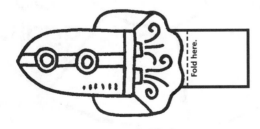
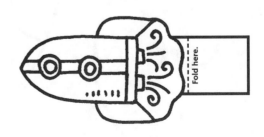

Fold here.

Math to the Moon

Game Board

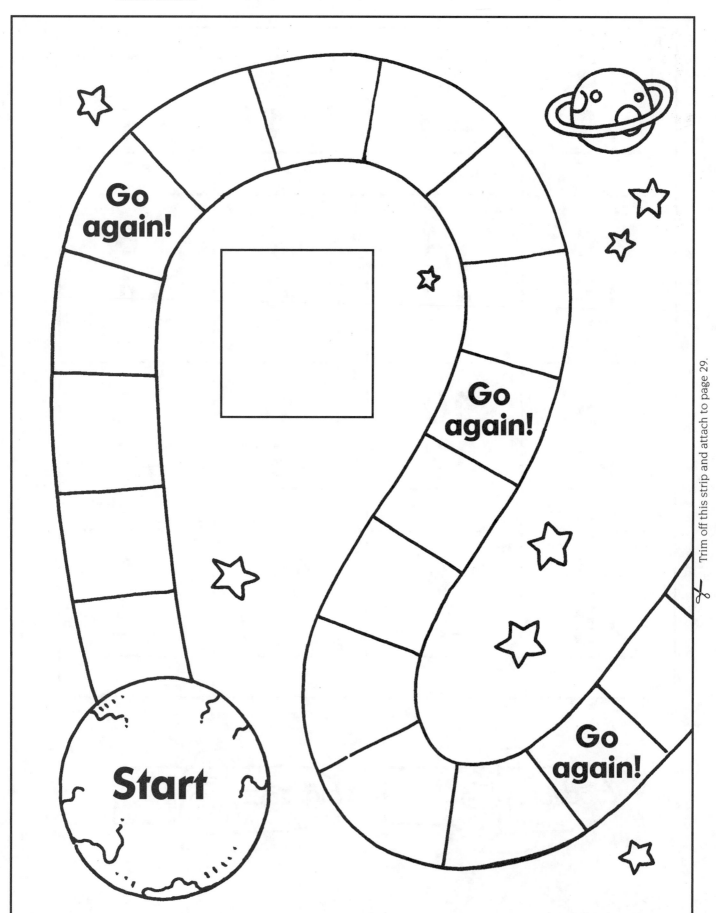

Go again!

Go again!

Go again!

Start

Trim off this strip and attach to page 29.

Math to the Moon

Game Board

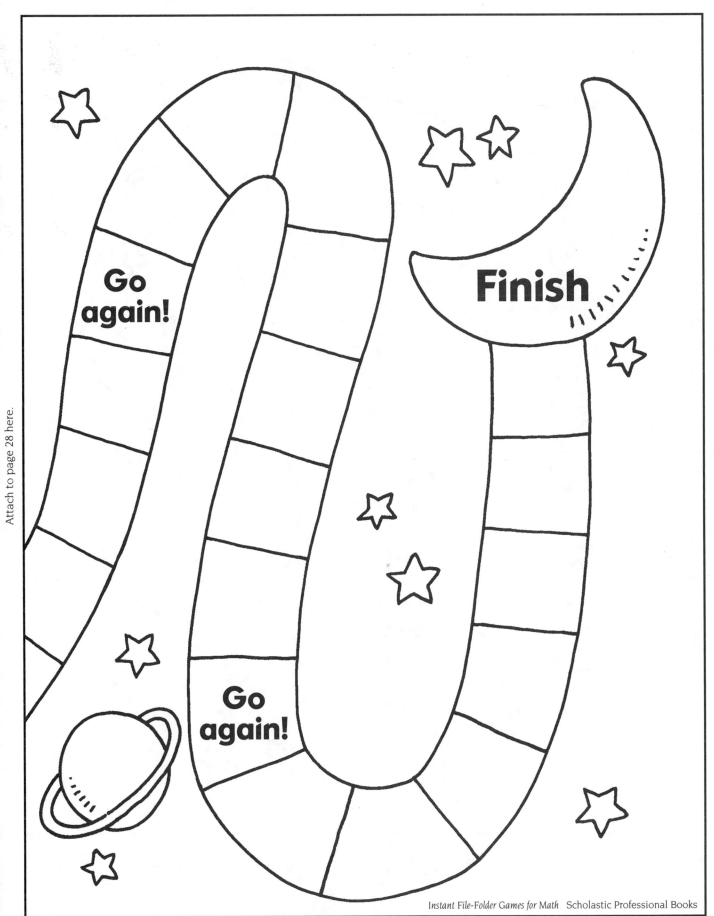

Go again!

Go again!

Finish

Instant File-Folder Games for Math   Scholastic Professional Books

Math to the Moon
Label and Pocket

Math to the Moon

Math to the Moon

Number Puzzles

Objective: This game provides practice in using place value and identifying even and odd numbers.

Introduction

You may wish to review with students place value for ones, tens, and hundreds.

Assembling the Game

 Duplicate and cut out the file-folder label and pocket on page 32. Glue the label onto the tab of a file folder. Tape the pocket on three sides to the outside front of the folder.

 Duplicate and cut out the directions and answer key on page 33. When the game is not in use, store these items in the pocket on the front of the folder.

 The game board consists of two puzzles: a giraffe and an elephant (pages 34–35). Make two copies of the giraffe on yellow paper and two copies of the elephant on blue paper. Glue one copy of each puzzle onto the inside of the folder. Cut apart the shapes on the second copy to make the pieces.

 Duplicate the spinner on page 36 and mount it on sturdy posterboard. (You can also laminate it.) To make the spinner, use a paper clip with either a brass fastener or a pencil to hold it in place. Unbend the end of a large paper clip and use it to punch a hole in the center of the spinner. Place the round end of the paper clip over the hole and attach it by inserting a brass fastener in the hole. Or show kids how to place the tip of a pencil in the center of the spinner and spin the paper clip around the pencil tip, as shown.

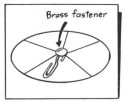

The Sturdy Way

The Fast and Easy Way

Extending the Game

⊙ Trace the puzzle patterns and write other numbers on the shapes to create additional puzzles.

⊙ Have students write how many ones, tens, and hundreds are in each number on the puzzle.

Number Puzzles

Directions for Play
(for 2 players)

1 Each player chooses one puzzle on the game board (the giraffe or the elephant) and takes the pieces of the same color as the puzzle. Players spread out their pieces with the numbers showing.

2 To take a turn, a player spins the spinner and reads the clue out loud. The player looks for a piece with a number that matches the clue. If the player finds a piece that matches, the player places it where it belongs on his or her puzzle. If the player cannot find a piece that matches a clue and fits on the puzzle, the turn ends.

3 Players continue to take turns. The first player to complete a puzzle wins.

Answer Key

Number greater than 50 but less than 99
54, 63, 68, 72, 81, 84, 89, 90

All of its digits add up to 9
54, 63, 72, 81, 90, 117, 171, 207, 333, 405, 540, 900

Three-digit odd number
101, 117, 171, 207, 285, 289, 333, 389, 405, 447, 507, 689, 697, 789, 809, 909, 987

Odd number with a 0 in the tens place
101, 207, 405, 507, 809, 909

Three-digit number with a 7 in the ones place
117, 207, 447, 507, 697, 987

Even number with a 9 in the hundreds place
900, 946, 966, 982

Odd number with an 8 in the tens place
81, 89, 285, 289, 389, 689, 789, 987

Number Puzzles

Giraffe Puzzle

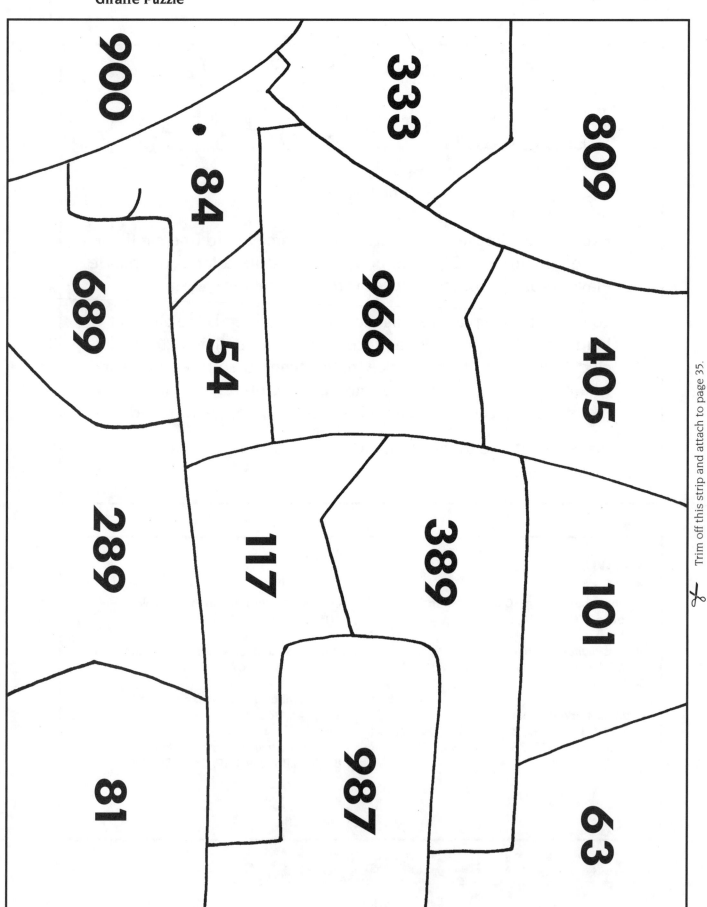

Trim off this strip and attach to page 35.

Number Puzzles

Elephant Puzzle

Attach to page 34 here.

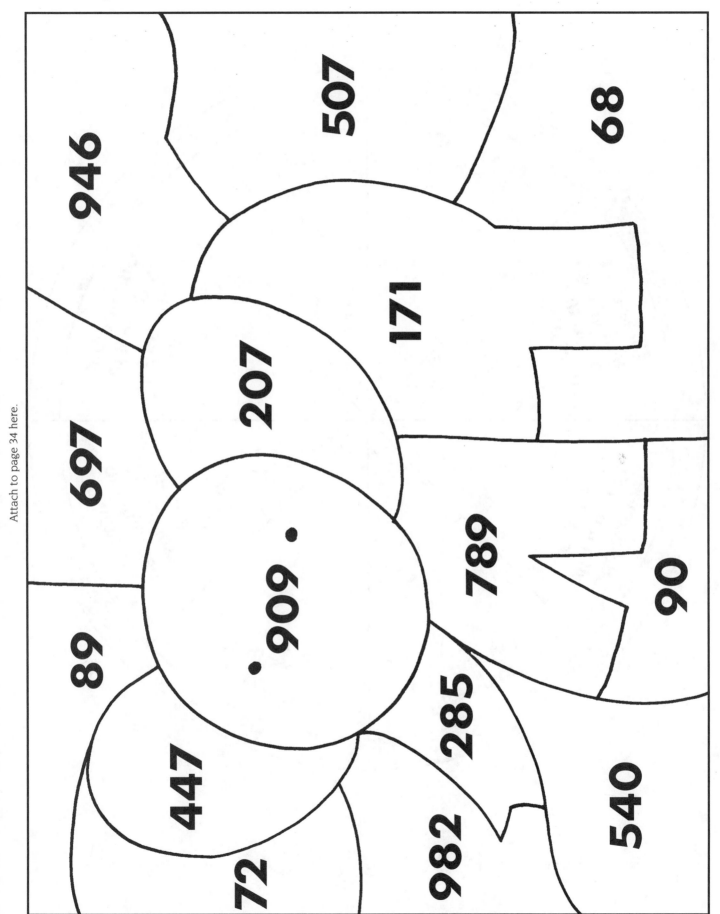

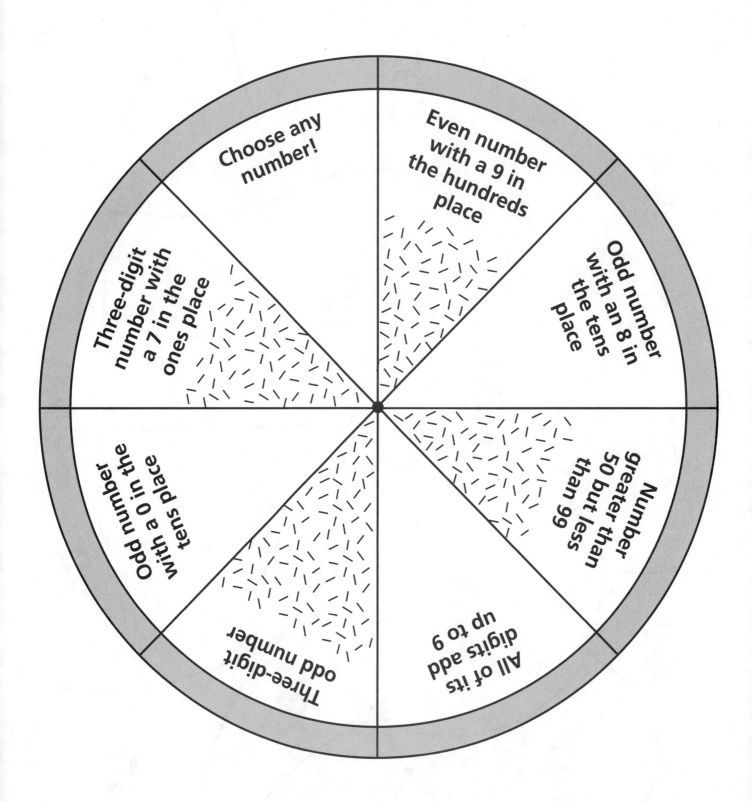

Choose any number!

Even number with a 9 in the hundreds place

Three-digit number with a 7 in the ones place

Odd number with an 8 in the tens place

Odd number with a 0 in the tens place

Number greater than 50 but less than 99

Three-digit odd number

All of its digits add up to 9

Pattern Play

Objective: This game provides practice in recognizing and forming patterns.

Introduction

Review two- or three-symbol patterns with students, such as A,B,C,A,B,C, and so on. Explain that a pattern is a design or arrangement that repeats.

Assembling the Game

 Duplicate and cut out the file-folder label and pocket on page 38. Glue the label onto the tab of a file folder. Tape the pocket on three sides to the outside front of the folder.

 Duplicate and cut out the answer key below and the directions and three sets of the picture cards on page 39. When the game is not in use, store these items in the pocket on the front of the folder.

 Duplicate and cut out the game boards on pages 40–41. Glue these onto the inside of the file folder so that Row 1 on each board is closest to the center.

 Invite students to color the game board and cards so that each type of shape is the same color. For example, color all the balloons red, all the flowers yellow, and so on.

Extending the Game

⊙ Challenge students to create additional patterns using the cards from the game or other manipulatives.

Answer Key

Game Board 1
Row 1: sun, fish, sun, fish, sun, fish
Row 2: star, flower, balloon, star, flower, balloon
Row 3: leaf, leaf, sun, sun, leaf, leaf
Row 4: heart, rainbow, rainbow, heart, rainbow, rainbow

Game Board 2
Row 1: leaf, flower, leaf, flower, leaf, flower
Row 2: star, heart, heart, star, heart, heart
Row 3: sun, balloon, rainbow, sun, balloon, rainbow
Row 4: fish, fish, flower, flower, fish, fish

Pattern Play

Pattern Play

Pattern Play

Directions for Play
(for 2 players)

1 Place the cards facedown in a pile. Players sit opposite each other and each chooses one side of the board. Players think about what shapes could fill the blanks to complete the patterns in each row.

2 One player picks the top card. If the picture on the card can fill in a blank, the player places the card in that spot. If not, the player places the card at the bottom of the pile.

3 Players take turn picking cards and filling in the blank spots on their patterns.

4 Play continues until one player has filled in all blank spots on his or her side of the board.

5 That player tells the order of shapes in his or her patterns.

Pattern Play

Game Board 1

Row 4	Row 3	Row 2	Row 1

Trim off this strip and attach to page 41.

Pattern Play
Game Board 2

Row 1

Row 2

Row 3

Row 4

Players: 2

Shapes for Sale

Objective: This game provides practice in identifying shapes and following directions.

Introduction

Have students review the attributes of the geometric shapes in this game (see shape cards on page 43).

Assembling the Game

1. Duplicate and cut out the file-folder label and pocket on page 46. Glue the label onto the tab of a file folder. Tape the pocket on three sides to the outside front of the folder.

2. Duplicate and cut out the answer key below and the directions and two sets of the shape cards on page 43. When the game is not in use, store these items in the pocket on the front of the folder.

3. Duplicate and cut out the game board on pages 44–45. Glue it onto the inside of the file folder.

4. Invite students to color the game board and shape cards.

   NOTE: This game requires a die or number cube (page 64) and playing pieces (chips, colored squares of paper, beans, and so on).

Extending the Game

⊙ Have students find objects or pictures of objects that are the same as the shapes on the cards.

Answer Key

1. pentagon	5. triangle	11. circle	16. diamond	22. circle
2. square, rectangle, or diamond	6. rectangle	12. square, rectangle, or diamond	17. oval	23. pentagon, hexagon, or octagon
	7. pentagon		18. hexagon	
3. triangle	8. octagon	13. triangle	19. square	24. hexagon
	9. half circle	14. octagon	20. half circle	25. circle
4. oval	10. rectangle	15. square	21. square, rectangle, or diamond	26. rectangle

Shapes for Sale

Directions for Play
(for 2 players)

 Each player takes 10 cards (one of each shape) and a playing piece.

 To take a turn, a player rolls the die, moves that number of spaces, and reads the description of the shape the shopper wants to buy. If the player has a card with that shape, the player covers that space with the card. (Some spaces have more than one possible answer. Players can only place one card per turn.) When moving around the board, players must skip over spaces that are covered with cards.

3 Players continue to take turns and move around the board until one player has "sold" all of his or her shapes.

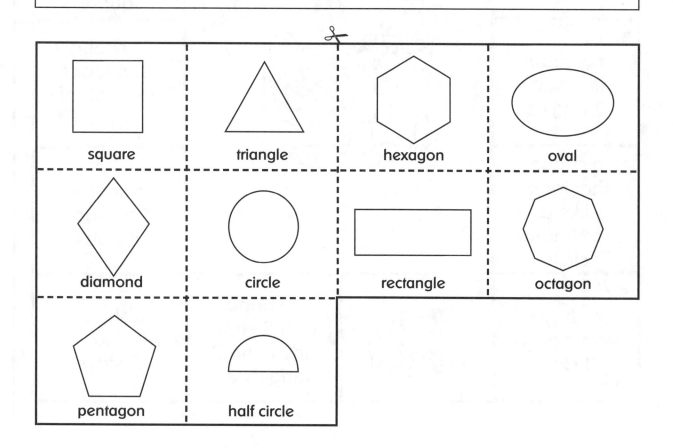

square	triangle	hexagon	oval
diamond	circle	rectangle	octagon
pentagon	half circle		

Shapes for Sale

Game Board

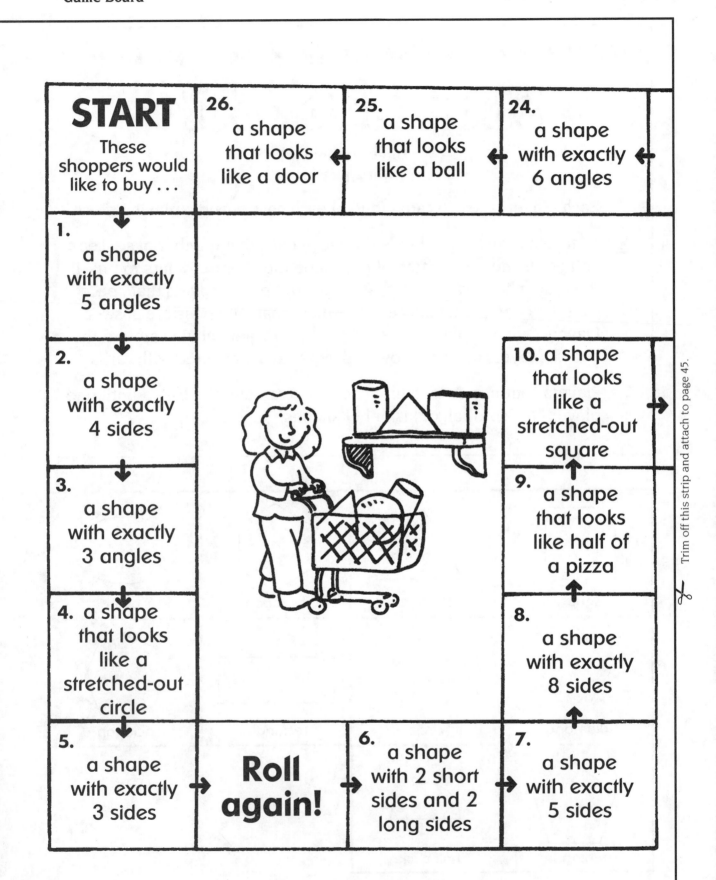

START
These shoppers would like to buy . . .

26. a shape that looks like a door

25. a shape that looks like a ball

24. a shape with exactly 6 angles

1. a shape with exactly 5 angles

2. a shape with exactly 4 sides

3. a shape with exactly 3 angles

4. a shape that looks like a stretched-out circle

5. a shape with exactly 3 sides

Roll again!

6. a shape with 2 short sides and 2 long sides

7. a shape with exactly 5 sides

8. a shape with exactly 8 sides

9. a shape that looks like half of a pizza

10. a shape that looks like a stretched-out square

Trim off this strip and attach to page 45.

Shapes for Sale

Game Board

23. a shape with 5 or more sides ←	**Roll again!** ←	**22.** a shape that looks like a record or CD ←	**21.** a shape with exactly 4 sides
			20. a shape that looks like half of a cookie ↑
11. a shape that looks like a pizza →	**12.** a shape with exactly 4 angles ↓		**19.** a shape with exactly 4 equal sides ↑
	Roll again! ↓		**18.** a shape with exactly 6 sides ↑
	13. a shape that looks like an ice cream cone ↓		**17.** a shape that looks like an egg ↑
	14. a shape with exactly 8 angles	**15.** a shape with exactly 4 equal sides →	**16.** a shape with the same name as a jewel →

Attach to page 44 here.

Shapes for Sale ▸▸

Label and Pocket

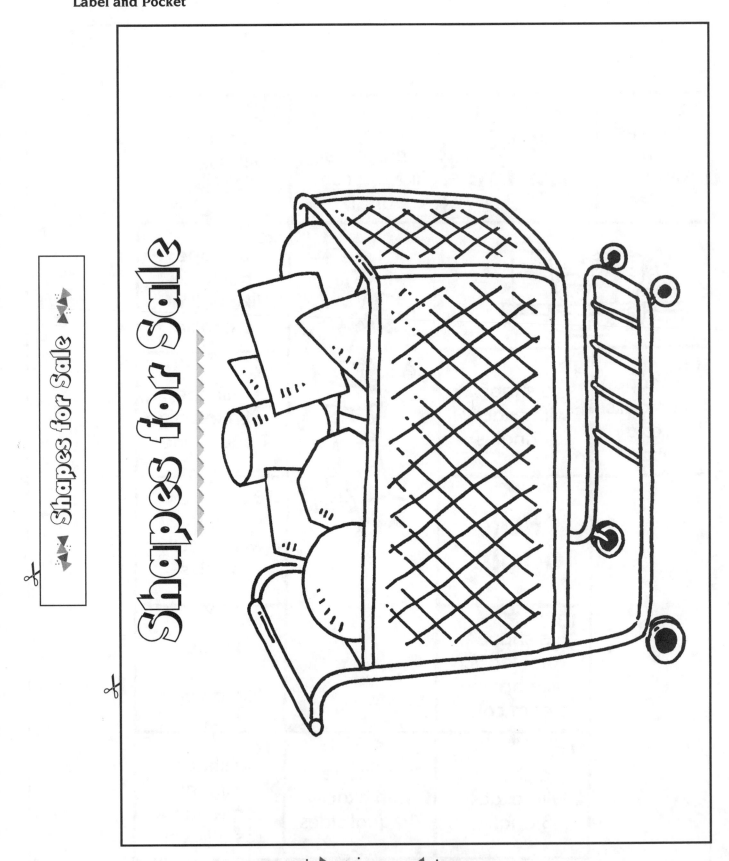

Shapes for Sale

Shapes for Sale

Fraction Fun

Objective: This game provides practice with simple fractions.

Introduction

Have students use manipulatives to review fractions.

Assembling the Game

 Duplicate and cut out the file-folder label and pocket on page 48. Glue the label onto the tab of a file folder. Tape the pocket on three sides to the outside front of the folder.

 Duplicate and cut out the directions and answer key on page 49. When the game is not in use, store these items in the pocket on the front of the folder.

 Make two copies of the game board on page 50. Glue them onto the inside of the file folder so that the pictures are facing the edges of the folder.

NOTE: This game requires paper and pencil for keeping score, two dice or number cubes (page 64), and two playing pieces (chips, colored squares of paper, beans, and so on).

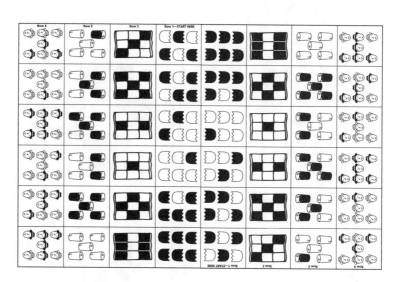

Extending the Game

⊙ Snack time is a great opportunity to practice fractions. Cut various snack foods into halves, fourths, and so on to demonstrate simple fractions.

Fraction Fun ▸▸

Label and Pocket

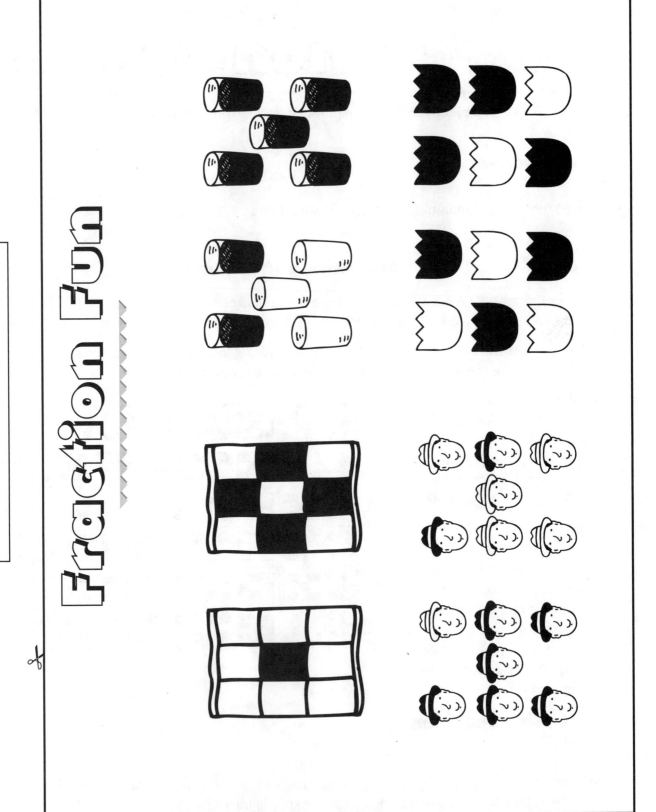

Fraction Fun

Directions for Play
(for 2 players)

1. Players sit opposite each other and each chooses one side of the game board.

2. Players set a target point total that wins the game, such as 30 points.

3. Players each take one die and roll at the same time. Starting in the top row, players move their pieces to the right the number of spaces that they rolled. Each player looks at the fraction picture and names the fraction. For example, if one out of six flowers is shaded, the player says, "One-sixth."

4. The player with the greatest fraction wins the round. The winner receives the number of points that he or she rolled on that turn. For example, if the player rolled a five, he or she records five points.

5. To start a new round, players move their pieces down a row and continue playing in the same way. Players should always be in the same row as each other. When players have completed all rows, they move back to the top row and continue playing.

6. The first player to reach the target point total wins.

Answer Key

Row 1	$3/6$ or $1/2$	$4/6$ or $2/3$	$2/6$ or $1/3$	$1/6$	$5/6$	$6/6$ or 1
Row 2	$3/9$ or $1/3$	$5/9$	$2/9$	$1/9$	$4/9$	$6/9$ or $2/3$
Row 3	$1/5$	$3/5$	$4/5$	$2/5$	$5/5$ or 1	$0/5$ or 0
Row 4	$3/7$	$1/7$	$6/7$	$2/7$	$4/7$	$5/7$

Fraction Fun

Game Board

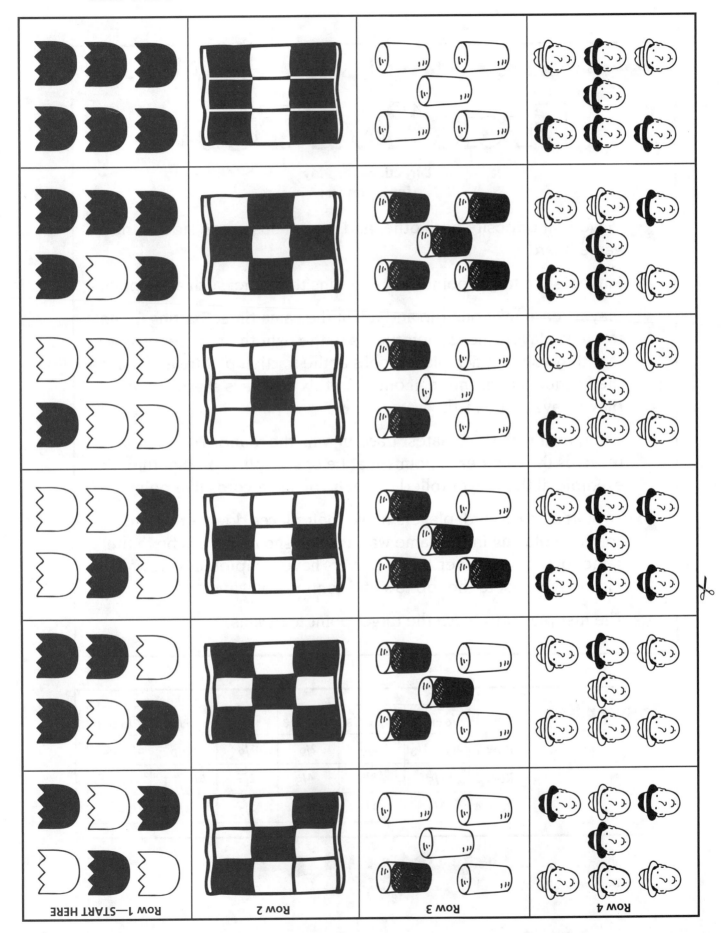

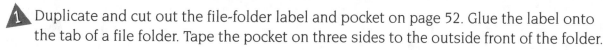

Objective: This game provides practice in counting money.

Introduction

You may wish to use play money to review coin and bill values with students before introducing the game. (You can use the reproducibles on page 56.)

Assembling the Game

1. Duplicate and cut out the file-folder label and pocket on page 52. Glue the label onto the tab of a file folder. Tape the pocket on three sides to the outside front of the folder.

2. Duplicate and cut out the directions on page 53. Make at least eight sets of the play money on page 56. Cut out the pieces, and glue together the fronts and backs of the coins. When the game is not in use, store these items in the pocket on the front of the folder.

3. Duplicate the game board on pages 54–55 and glue it onto the inside of the folder.

4. Invite students to color the game parts.

   NOTE: This game requires a die or number cube and playing pieces (chips, colored paper squares, beans, and so on).

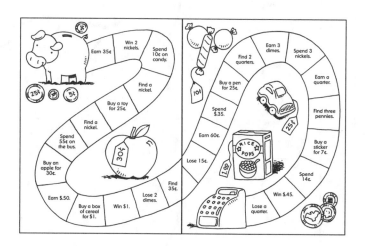

Extending the Game

⊙ Set up a play store in your classroom by labeling objects with price tags. Supply play money, pencils, and paper. Have students take turns being the cashier. Show students how to write receipts for items purchased.

Spend 'n Earn ▶▶

Label and Pocket

Spend 'n Earn

Directions for Play
(for 2–4 players)

1 Players place their pieces on Start and each take $2.25 in any combination of play bills and coins. The rest of the money is used for the "bank."

2 The first player rolls the die and moves that number of spaces. The player reads the directions on that space out loud and follows them. If the directions are to buy an item or lose money, the player puts the correct amount of money in the bank. (Players can also make change if needed.) If the player earns money, the player takes the correct amount from the bank. The turn ends and the next player takes a turn.

3 Players continue to take turns until they have all reached Finish or run out of money. The player with the most money is the winner. A player can also win if all the other players run out of money.

Spend 'n Earn

Game Board

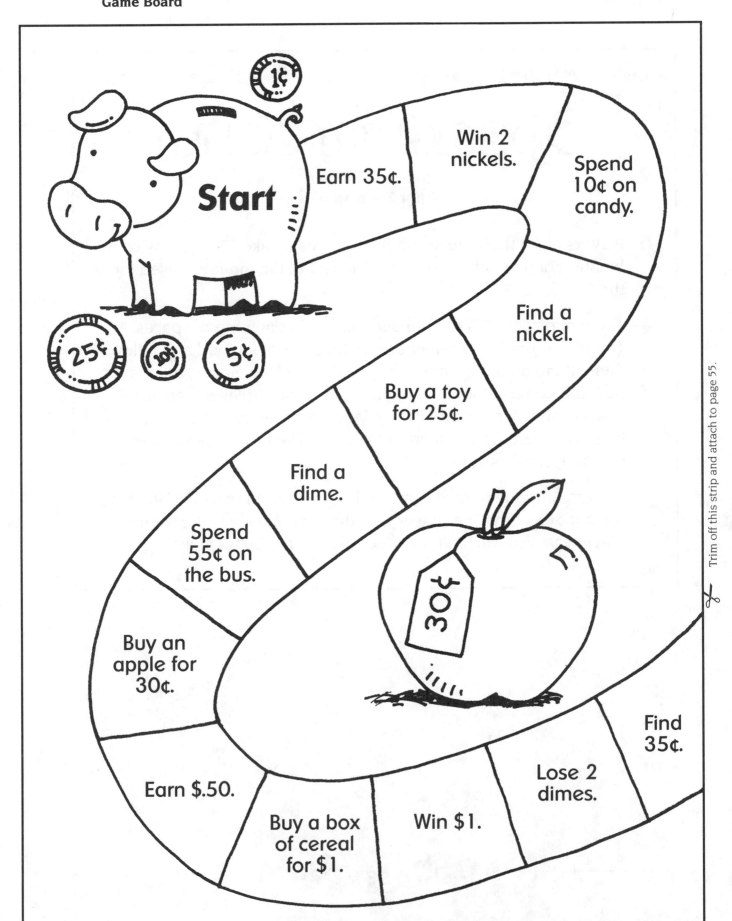

Start

Earn 35¢.

Win 2 nickels.

Spend 10¢ on candy.

Find a nickel.

Buy a toy for 25¢.

Find a dime.

Spend 55¢ on the bus.

Buy an apple for 30¢.

30¢

Earn $.50.

Buy a box of cereal for $1.

Win $1.

Lose 2 dimes.

Find 35¢.

1¢

25¢

10¢

5¢

Trim off this strip and attach to page 55.

Spend 'n Earn

Game Board

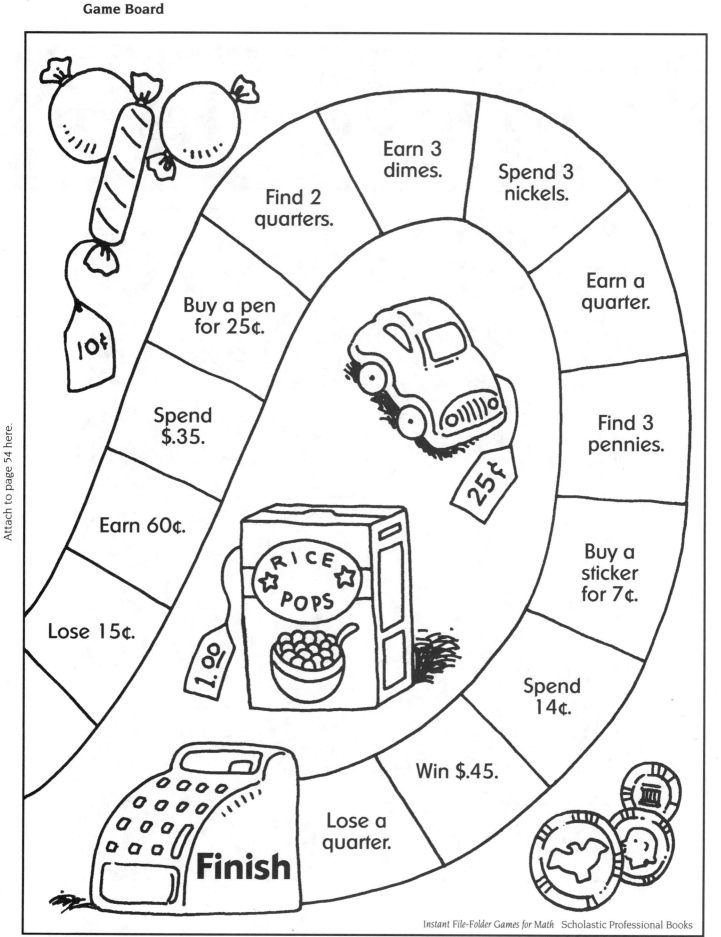

Find 2 quarters.

Earn 3 dimes.

Spend 3 nickels.

Buy a pen for 25¢.

Earn a quarter.

Spend $.35.

Find 3 pennies.

Earn 60¢.

RICE POPS

1.00

25¢

Buy a sticker for 7¢.

Lose 15¢.

Spend 14¢.

Win $.45.

Lose a quarter.

10¢

Finish

Spend 'n Earn
Money Reproducibles

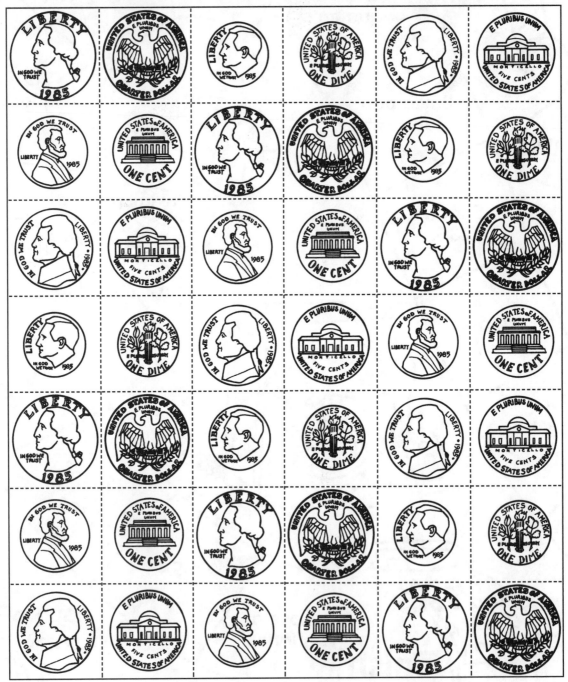

Objective: This game provides practice with multiplication.

Introduction

You may wish to review multiplication facts before showing students how to play the game.

Assembling the Game

 Duplicate and cut out the file-folder label and pocket on page 58. Glue the label onto the tab of a file folder. Tape the pocket on three sides to the outside front of the folder.

 Duplicate and cut out the directions, cards, and answer key on pages 59–61. When the game is not in use, store these items in the pocket on the front of the folder.

 Copy the playing pieces on page 61, and cut them out. Color the clothing on each a different color. Fold the bottom so that the pieces stand.

 Duplicate and cut out the game board on pages 62–63. Invite students to color it, and then glue it onto the inside of the file folder.

Extending the Game

⊙ Make additional cards with other multiplication problems. You can also make addition, subtraction, or division cards to use with this game.

Multiplication Mountain

Multiplication Mountain

Multiplication Mountain

Directions for Play
(for 2 players)

1. Each player places a playing piece on Start. Place the cards face-down in a pile.

2. Each player picks a card, reads the problem out loud, and says the answer. Players can check their answers with the answer key, if necessary.

3. The player with the greater answer moves ahead one space. If the answers are the same, both players move ahead one space. Players then place their cards at the bottom of the pile.

4. The first player to reach Finish wins.

Answer Key

1. $0 \times 9 = 0$	10. $5 \times 3 = 15$	19. $8 \times 4 = 32$	28. $7 \times 6 = 42$
2. $1 \times 8 = 8$	11. $3 \times 6 = 18$	20. $4 \times 9 = 36$	29. $6 \times 8 = 48$
3. $5 \times 2 = 10$	12. $7 \times 3 = 21$	21. $5 \times 5 = 25$	30. $9 \times 6 = 54$
4. $2 \times 6 = 12$	13. $3 \times 8 = 24$	22. $5 \times 6 = 30$	31. $7 \times 7 = 49$
5. $7 \times 2 = 14$	14. $9 \times 3 = 27$	23. $5 \times 7 = 35$	32. $8 \times 7 = 56$
6. $2 \times 8 = 16$	15. $4 \times 4 = 16$	24. $8 \times 5 = 40$	33. $7 \times 9 = 63$
7. $9 \times 2 = 18$	16. $4 \times 5 = 20$	25. $5 \times 9 = 45$	34. $8 \times 8 = 64$
8. $3 \times 3 = 9$	17. $6 \times 4 = 24$	26. $6 \times 5 = 30$	35. $8 \times 9 = 72$
9. $3 \times 4 = 12$	18. $4 \times 7 = 28$	27. $6 \times 6 = 36$	36. $9 \times 9 = 81$

Multiplication Mountain
Cards

1. **0 x 9**	2. **1 x 8**	3. **5 x 2**	4. **2 x 6**
5. **7 x 2**	6. **2 x 8**	7. **9 x 2**	8. **3 x 3**
9. **3 x 4**	10. **5 x 3**	11. **3 x 6**	12. **7 x 3**
13. **3 x 8**	14. **9 x 3**	15. **4 x 4**	16. **4 x 5**
17. **6 x 4**	18. **4 x 7**	19. **8 x 4**	20. **4 x 9**

Multiplication Mountain

Cards and Playing Pieces

21. **5 x 5**	22. **5 x 6**	23. **5 x 7**	24. **8 x 5**
25. **5 x 9**	26. **6 x 5**	27. **6 x 6**	28. **7 x 6**
29. **6 x 8**	30. **9 x 6**	31. **7 x 7**	32. **8 x 7**
33. **7 x 9**	34. **8 x 8**	35. **8 x 9**	36. **9 x 9**

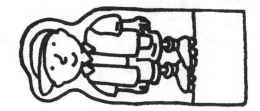 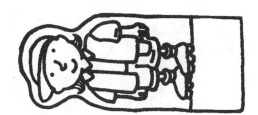

Multiplication Mountain

Game Board

FINISH

Trim off this strip and attach to page 63.

Multiplication Mountain

Game Board

Instant File-Folder Games for Math   Scholastic Professional Books

Attach to page 62 here.

START

Number Cubes

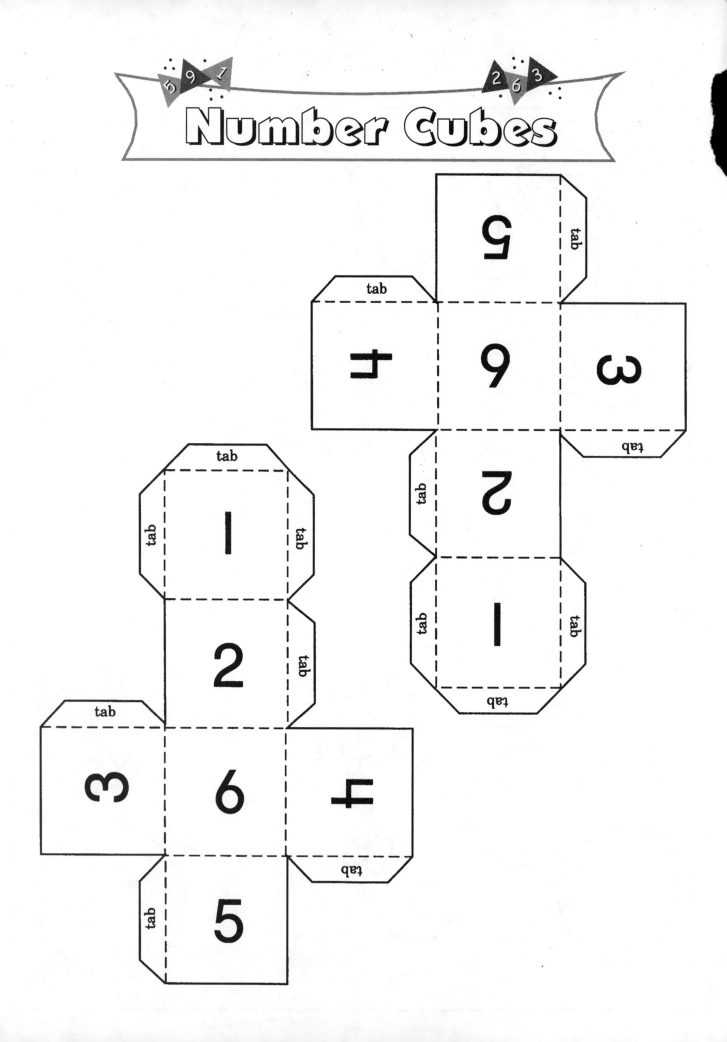